Golden Retriever

By Nona Kilgore Bauer

8/13

BREEDERS' BEST
A KENNEL CLUB BOOK™

GOLDEN RETRIEVER

ISBN: 1-59378-902-5

Copyright © 2004
Kennel Club Books, LLC
308 Main Street, Allenhurst, NJ 0711 USA
Printed in South Korea

10 9 8 7 6 5 4 3 2 1

PHOTOS BY:
Isabelle Français
and Bernd Brinkmann.

DRAWINGS BY:
Yolyanko el Habanero.

Contents

Meet the Golden Retriever

Whoever said "you can't have it all" never met the Golden Retriever. From a superb waterfowl retriever at the turn of the 20th century, the Golden has morphed into a do-everything dog that excels in every area of canine service. Today's Golden Retriever guides the blind, assists the handicapped, sniffs out drugs and explosives, locates people buried in the rubble of earthquakes and other disasters and comforts both young and old in hospitals and nursing homes. And let's not forget

The Golden Retriever is one of the most popular companion dogs in the world as well as talented at his intended purpose and widely used by hunters.

his most important role, that of best friend and sometime hunting partner to his human family. Small wonder we see a smiling Golden Retriever face on everything from greeting cards to cereal boxes to sweatshirts.

Surely the man behind the original Golden had no idea of the 14-karat empire he was founding. The first Lord Tweedmouth of Guisachan (the former Sir Dudley Marjoriebanks) dreamed simply of a superior yellow retriever who would fetch his ducks from the icy waters of the Tweed River near the coast of Scotland. To that end, Tweedmouth, in 1868, launched an ambitious breeding program with the mating of his yellow Wavy-Coated Retriever named Nous (who was out of a litter of all-black pups, ancestors of today's Flat-Coated Retriever) and a Tweed Water Spaniel bitch named Belle. The Tweed Water Spaniel was a favored hunting dog, known for its intelligence,

When you think of the Golden, do you think of the wolf? Probably not, but all dogs can trace their origins back to this common ancestor.

The Golden loves the water and is a natural-born swimmer. He's as skilled at retrieving in the water as he is on land, with a protective water-repellent coat that allows him to work in all types of weather conditions.

superior swimming ability and biddable temperament. From that pairing came four fuzzy yellow pups who were to become the ancestors of the versatile Golden Retriever we know and love today.

Tweedmouth kept one yellow pup and dubbed it Cowslip, and gave the other three to friends who shared his "golden" vision. Tweedmouth's breeding program focused on "fixing" the yellow gene in a water-loving retriever of exceptional temperament. The offspring resulting from his matings and those of his associates continued to produce Golden-type hunting dogs that were highly prized for their great courage, sagacity and temperament. Historians of that era wrote also of the breed's unique ability to bond to humans: "He rivals every other breed in his attachment to his master," surely an apt description of our modern Golden Retriever.

Golden Retrievers were first registered in the UK with The Kennel Club in 1903 in the general category of Retrievers. In 1913, they were recognized as "Yellow or Golden Retrievers;" the term "Yellow" was officially dropped in 1920.

The breed migrated to the United States in the early 1900s and gained official American Kennel Club (AKC) recognition in 1925. The early Goldens were known to be powerful and courageous hunting dogs that hunted hard while also competing in the show ring. Distinct separation between the hunting-dog type and the show dog did not occur until the breed rode the popularity wave during the 1950s.

Thanks to Tweedmouth's passion for an intelligent and biddable retriever, the 21st-century Golden has retained many of the qualities that its founder most valued. Although most Goldens today spend more time romping in the family room than in the duck blind, they are still considered a most capable dog to hunt over, compete with or just live with and hug a lot.

Today's Golden Retriever surely excels at huggability. There are no strangers with this breed, as a Golden will greet every human being with the same enthusiasm as he would a long-time friend. Such affability has made the Golden the ideal candidate for therapy work in hospitals and nursing homes.

As a guide and assistance dog, the Golden has no peer. His ability to bond with a human partner is legendary. In search-and-rescue work, the Golden has labored valiantly during many disasters, notably the September 11, 2001 tragedy, demonstrating that the courage of his ancestors still runs strong.

In the field, many Goldens still prove their worth as hunting dogs. They consistently demonstrate their superior nose on upland game and retrieve waterfowl in sub-zero weather. They also excel in hunting tests and trials, and very demanding field-trial competitions.

Few breeds surpass the Golden's zest for life. The Golden finds joy in every moment of the day, exploring every hole and corner of the yard with the enthusiasm of Columbus discovering America,

The Golden's talents have extended well beyond the field, as the breed has come to be used in many areas of canine service. As an assistance dog, the Golden is a loyal companion and helper, performing tasks for his physically challenged owner.

retrieving sticks that are twice his size.

Goldens are known to be very "oral" dogs that love to mouth an arm or hand from sheer enthusiasm. They will find and retrieve anything within their reach, especially socks and other articles of

CHAPTER

clothing. Unchecked, they will shred these things up. Conscientious owners quickly learn to keep everything off the floor and wait for their Goldens to mature (don't hold your breath!).

The beauty of the luxurious Golden Retriever coat is a mixed blessing, as it sheds twice a year in fluffy clouds of doggie down. Golden owners devote large blocks of time each week to grooming their dogs, brushing that thick golden coat and vacuuming the furniture. Persnickety housekeepers should investigate other breeds.

As a sporting dog and natural athlete, the Golden requires vigorous exercise. If those requirements are not met, the breed will redirect its energy into "fun" things like

Two hallmarks of the Golden Retriever: his beautiful flowing golden coat and his oral fixation. As a retriever, the Golden is rarely without something in his mouth, so owners must provide plenty of safe options.

digging up your garden or remodeling your furniture. Their sociability factor is high, and they will not thrive as an outside dog that is separated from its family.

The Golden Retriever is considered a medium- to large-sized breed, with males 23–24 inches at the withers and weighing 65–75 pounds; females 21.5–22.5. inches and 55–65 pounds.

For the past 20 years, the Golden Retriever has placed consistently in the top five breeds registered with the AKC. Unfortunately, such popularity has a price. As happens with all dog breeds that captivate the public's eye, the modern Golden is a sorry victim of mass-market and "backyard" breeders who produce Goldens in quantity. These are poor-quality dogs that are irritable and unhealthy, aggressive with other dogs and sometimes people. Not to mention, these breeders are producing Golden Retrievers that lack a basic desire to retrieve. In yet another scenario, "specialty" breeders, in an effort to produce dogs that excel in field work, obedience or confor- mation, have sacrificed the all- around good nature of the Golden to pursue top-winning dogs in their particular specialties.

That said, breeder selection is of the utmost importance when shopping for a Golden puppy. Puppy buyers must sort through those breeders who produce atypical or unhealthy Goldens. To do otherwise, one risks facing a host of health problems such as hip and elbow dysplasia, which lead to early arthritis, lameness and big vet bills; allergies and thyroid problems (more big vet bills); or temperament problems like aggression or hyperactivity, which can lead to dangerous or destructive behavior.

MEET THE GOLDEN RETRIEVER

Overview

- The Golden Retriever is known to excel as an all-around companion, competition, field and service dog.
- Lord Tweedmouth, the originator of the breed, had intentions of producing a talented water retriever capable of performing in icy conditions.
- The original breeding program fixed many desirable qualities in the Golden, including beauty, hunting skills, intelligence, versatility, wonderful temperament and unmatched loyalty.
- Today Lord Tweedmouth's "yellow retriever" is one of the world's most popular companion breeds. Unfortunately, popularity has led to mass breeding; additionally, there is some diversion in type among field and show dogs. Owners should seek sound typical Goldens produced by reputable breeders.

Description of the Golden

The official standard of a dog breed describes in great detail the many qualities that make that breed distinct in conformation, ability and character. Written by the breed's parent club, the Golden Retriever Club of America, the breed standard sets forth guidelines used by judges in evaluating breed specimens and by breeders in planning their breeding programs. Using this "blueprint," breeders strive to produce dogs that are exemplary specimens of the breed. Without such guidelines, the Golden Retriever could eventually lose all those qualities that make it "golden."

The Golden's nature is reflected in his trademark expression, which should be "kindly" and showing a "personality that is eager, alert and self-confident."

The Golden was originally developed as a hunting dog. The breed standard, by addressing that purpose in its very first paragraph, "General Appearance," emphasizes the importance of the "retriever" in the Golden: "A symmetrical, powerful, active dog, sound and well put together, not clumsy nor long in the leg, displaying a kindly expression and possessing a personality that is eager, alert and self-confident. Primarily a hunting dog, he should be shown in hard working condition. Overall appearance, balance, gait and purpose to be given more emphasis than any of his component parts."

Even Golden Retrievers who do not hunt (most Goldens today) should still have hunting instinct and be true to the standard—athletic, muscular and in hard-working physical condition. The Golden also must be well put together in order to partake in high-energy sporting activities, whether

The Golden is a natural beauty, but his coat is foremost functional. The water-repellent double coat is the ideal insulation and protection for work in water and afield.

A top-quality Golden fully groomed for the show ring. True Golden fanciers aim to produce all-around dogs with the balance of form, function and temperament that enables them to succeed at work, in the ring and in the home.

CHAPTER 2

competition or backyard tennis-ball-fetching.

Size and proportion are important to the overall character of the Golden, with males 23 to 24 inches at the withers (shoulders) and females 21.5 to 22.5 inches. Length from the breastbone to the point of buttocks is slightly greater than the height at withers in a ratio of 12:11. Ideal weight for dogs ranges from 65 to 75 pounds; bitches, 55 to 65 pounds.

Today one may see Goldens who are several inches taller than the standard and/or weigh in excess of 90 pounds. Dogs of such stature are not representative of the Golden Retriever as a sporting animal and should not be bred. A poorly structured retriever would be unable to spend the day afield retrieving and carrying upland game and waterfowl.

The classic Golden Retriever head and expression are prized hallmarks of the breed. The eyes mirror the soul of the breed…"friendly and intelligent in expression." "Friendly" is again addressed in the section on temperament: "Friendly, reliable and trustworthy. Quarrelsomeness or hostility towards other dogs or people in normal situations, or an unwarranted show of timidity or nervousness, is not in keeping with Golden Retriever character."

The Golden's coat is as utilitarian as it is huggable, serving as protection from both heat and cold and from potentially damaging underbrush when hunting upland game. Although color extremes are undesirable, Golden coat colors range from dark red to very pale blond. Coat color is simply a matter of personal preference.

The Golden's characteristic love-everyone affability is perhaps the breed's most defining quality. Such was the original yellow dog who hunted with Lord Tweedmouth. Goldens who are cranky or unpredictably hostile are not typical of the breed and should be excluded from breeding programs and avoided by prospective puppy buyers.

Of course, the "ideal" or perfect Golden Retriever is in reality a myth. And because of the split between show, field and obedience lines, many Goldens today are not even "typical." Rather, they are "specialists" who are bred for a breeder's particular focus or passion. Field dogs are bred for those qualities that enhance the dog afield, with less concern for some physical properties that are uniquely Golden. Breeders of show dogs focus on those features that will bring blue ribbons in the show ring, with little or no emphasis on hunting ability. Obedience competitors breed dogs that best serve their particular passion. Few find a middle ground and bend to the priorities of other specialists.

Fortunately, the majority of Goldens today are still great all-around dogs. Their multi-purpose roles and love of people are testaments to the dogs that Lord Tweedmouth cherished.

DESCRIPTION OF THE GOLDEN

Overview

- All Goldens should be athletic, muscular and well put together, capable of a hard day's work in the field whether or not they are actually used for hunting.
- The Golden's temperament is a breed hallmark. This is a friendly, outgoing, loving breed in which aggression and shyness are highly atypical and serious faults.
- The Golden's gorgeous coat is both protective and beautiful, ranging in shade from pale blond to rich reddish-gold.
- A typical Golden is well balanced, true to Lord Tweedmouth's vision, not a product of breeder whims and preferences.

CHAPTER 3

Are You a Golden Person?

If you are thinking golden thoughts, you should first take a step back and decide what kind of dog you're looking for before your puppy search begins. Golden Retrievers might be all-around, do-it-all dogs, but that does not mean that they're right for every dog lover. Part of the Golden Retriever's intrigue is that no two Goldens are alike. Of course, every dog has his own distinct personality, but in a breed as versatile as the Golden, one can find

A true family dog, a Golden Retriever loves to snuggle up with those he loves, which is just about everyone!

individuals with extreme differences in personality and ability.

Regardless, all Goldens are, or should be, people-loving fellows who greet both friend and stranger like long-lost buddies. They live best indoors with their families and will not thrive if isolated from the humans they so love. Contrary to some images of the "typical" Golden, these are high-energy sporting dogs that require a great deal of daily attention and exercise. They enjoy lively outdoor fun and games, which are excellent outlets for their energy and enthusiasm. Are your disposition and lifestyle compatible with those needs?

The Golden is known to be a "mouthy" creature who loves to carry something…anything…in his mouth, and that includes your hand, arm, socks and anything else not nailed down. He will happily retrieve your jockey shorts and deliver them to

A toy to chew, water to splash in and family members to spend time with—what more does a Golden need?

A Golden without enough to do means a Golden who will find something to do. Boredom in an active dog is asking for trouble!

your pastor when he visits. Only many months of training will redirect that oral instinct into proper behavior.

Chewing is a natural by-product of retrieving, and Golden puppies are miniature chewing machines. Many chew their way well into adulthood, leaving telltale scars on the furniture and cabinetry. A wise owner can minimize the damage with diligent supervision, providing appropriate chew toys and teaching the Golden puppy what he may and may not chew.

Owners who fail to dog-proof their homes or supervise their puppies tell horror stories about the impossible things their Goldens have consumed or destroyed. If you are not willing to train your pup or supervise him, be prepared to face the consequences.

Golden Retrievers are great with children, although Goldens can be especially exuberant, so both dog and kids must be supervised to prevent mishaps due to normal Golden rowdiness.

Will dog hair on your suit and sofa drive you wild? The fuzzy charm of a Golden puppy will blossom into a thick long coat that will require frequent brushing to keep it clean and loose hairs off your dinner plate. Goldens lose their heavy undercoat in spring, again in fall, and shed a little every day, all year long. Only regular brushing will keep that dog hair around the home to a minimum. And don't forget those muddy paws, tromping through your garden and across your kitchen floor. Few Golden Retriever homes have spotless tiled floors.

Potential Golden owners should consider their prefer-ences and needs before deciding on a dog and breeder. The split between field, show and obedience lines has created Goldens

A Golden owner must be prepared for an enthusiastic dog that just loves to be close to his loved ones.

CHAPTER 3

with marked differences in temperament, hunting ability and structure. The field Golden, who is bred for hunting, is generally leaner and less coated, often with a narrower head and a higher energy level. The Golden who has been bred to win blue ribbons in the show ring is typically heavier boned, with

overwhelm a novice owner who is unprepared for the breed's natural vigor and vitality. Perhaps due to Goldens' high public profile, many people are unaware that, while highly trainable, the Golden still requires training. He is more than anxious to please his person, but he needs to learn how to

An ideal living situation for a Golden is a home with a good-sized fenced yard and someone to throw a ball for him to retrieve.

shorter legs and a noticeably broader skull. The show Golden is usually more laid-back and less intense, if intense at all, in the field.

However, even a show-bred Golden puppy can be a handful. His enthusiasm and zest for life can easily

do that. Obedience training is the commonsense route to transforming an exuberant Golden into a well-behaved canine good citizen.

Golden rescue groups (breed organizations that rehome abandoned Goldens) routinely deal with disenchanted owners who give up their Goldens because of temperament and behavior problems. Quite simply, the dogs were never trained or poorly trained at best. Fortunately, many stout-hearted Golden owners who fail to train their dogs learn to tolerate and adjust to their Goldens' unruly ways because they love their dogs. Most likely, one of those dogs lives just down the street!

Breed and breeder selection are weighty

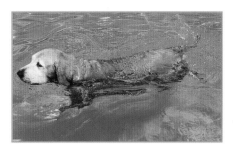

Landlocked? No problem! For a Golden, a dip in the family pool is just as good as swimming in the lake.

decisions and should be based on what's best for both you and your future dog. All this and more should determine whether or not you and a Golden Retriever could live happily ever after.

ARE YOU A GOLDEN PERSON?

Overview

- A Golden person enjoys a versatile talented dog that can join him and his family in many different activities.
- A Golden person wants to make his dog a true part of the family, as this is a dog with a loving temperament and devotion his people, thriving on the companionship of his human pack.
- A Golden person can deal with a high-energy dog as well as the oral tendencies shared by all retrievers.
- A Golden person will devote time to grooming his dog all year round and even more so during the spring and fall shedding seasons.
- A Golden person knows that training is necessary to direct his dog's talents and energy into good behavior and positive pursuits.

CHAPTER 4

Selecting a Breeder

A litter of Golden puppies should not be hard to find, since there seems to be at least one Golden on every block. Finding a reputable breeder, however, may not be as easy.

Whatever your reasons for wanting a Golden...family pet, competition dog or field companion, you want a healthy dog with a good disposition, a dog that looks and acts like the traditional Golden Retriever. Finding a breeder you can trust, who has experience with the breed and who raises quality Golden puppies, is

Don't choose a breeder unless her love of the breed is undeniably evident.

paramount and may take time, but a good pup is worth the extra effort.

A breeder-puppy search can be an emotionally trying experience, taxing your patience and your willpower. All puppies are adorable and it's easy to fall in love with the first cute pup you see, but a poor-quality Golden will have health and temperament problems that can empty your wallet and break your heart. So do your breeder homework before you visit those cute pups. Arm yourself with a list of questions for the breeder. Then leave your wallet and your kids at home so you aren't tempted to take home a poorly-bred but nonetheless irresistible Golden pup.

A good breeder starts early socialization with the litter, allowing them time to experience the world outdoors when they are old enough.

How will you resist? Do your breeder homework and select a reputable breeder before you go visiting the pups; otherwise, you're likely to lose your heart to the first adorable ball of golden fluff you see!

PEDIGREE AND REGISTRATION PAPERS

For starters, always ask to see the pup's pedigree and registration papers. Although AKC registration is no guarantee of quality, it is one small step in the right direction. And if you hope to show your pup or enter licensed competition, registration with the AKC is necessary.

The pedigree should include three to five generations of ancestry. Inquire about any titles in the pedigree. Titles indicate a dog's accomplishments in some area of canine competition, which proves the merits of the ancestors and adds to the breeder's credibility. You should see "Ch." in a show puppy's pedigree, indicating champion relatives. If yours is a field puppy, you should see an "AFC" or "MH," which stands for Amateur Field Champion or Master Hunter. While it is true that, like the registration, a pedigree cannot guarantee ability, health or good temperament, a well-constructed pedigree is still a good starting point.

There should be no extra fee, by the way, for either the pedigree or registration papers.

The AKC states that papers do not cost extra, and any breeder who charges for those documents is unscrupulous.

WHY THIS BREEDING?
Ask why the breeder planned this litter. A conscientious breeder plans a litter of Goldens for specific reasons and should explain the genetics behind this particular breeding and what he expects the breeding to produce. He never has pups because "his Golden is sweet and/or beautiful, his neighbor's dog is handsome, they will have lovely puppies," or "his kids needed to experience puppy birth" and so on. Just loving his dog like crazy does not qualify an individual to breed dogs intelligently or properly raise a litter of Golden pups.

Responsible breeders, by the way, do not raise several different breeds of dog or produce multiple litters of pups throughout the year. One or two litters a year is typical.

HEALTH ISSUES

Ask about health issues and the appropriate clearances. Goldens are prone to hip and elbow dysplasia and osteo-chondritis dissecans (OCD), three hereditary and poten-tially crippling joint diseases. Do the sire and dam have hip and elbow clearances from the OFA (Orthopedic Foundation for Animals, a national canine genetic disease registry)? Have the parents' eyes been examined for progressive retinal atrophy (PRA) and cataracts within the past year by a board-certified veterinary ophthalmologist? Eye clear-ances can be registered with the Canine Eye Registry Foundation (CERF). Good breeders will gladly provide those documents.

Other health problems recognized in the Golden include epilepsy, thyroid disorders and allergies. You can research these and other Golden health problems through the breed's parent club, the Golden Retriever Club of America, at www.grca.org, and canine health websites.

BREED INVOLVEMENT

Experienced Golden breeders are frequently involved in some aspect of the dog fancy with their dog(s), perhaps showing in conformation, competing in hunt tests or field trials or training for other performance events or dog-

From quality breeding come quality puppies. The goal of every good breeder should be to breed only top-quality dogs with clean bills of health in order to pass on the best traits of the breed to each generation.

related activities. Their Golden(s) may have earned titles in competition, which is added proof of the breeder's experience and commitment to the breed.

Dedicated breeders often

CHAPTER 4

belong to the Golden Retriever Club of America (GRCA) and/or a local breed or kennel club. Such affiliation with other experienced breeders and sportsmen expands their knowledge of their chosen breed, which further enhances their credibility.

MORE FROM THE BREEDER

The breeder will ask you questions, too… about your dog history, previous dogs you have owned, what breeds of dog and

and your family are suitable owners who will provide a proper and loving home for one of his precious little ones. You should be suspicious of any breeder who agrees to sell you a Golden puppy without any type of interrogation or interview process. Such indifference indicates a lack of concern about the pups and casts doubt on the breeder's ethics and breeding program.

A good breeder also will warn you about the downside

Not all Goldens will make it to the breed ring at the Westminster Kennel Club show, but involvement in some area of the canine sport is a testament to the breeder's dedication.

what became of those dogs. He will want to know your living arrangements, i.e., house, yard, kids, other pups, etc., your goals for this pup and how you plan to raise him. The breeder's primary concern is the future of his puppies and whether you

of the Golden Retriever. No breed of dog is perfect, nor is every breed suitable for every person's temperament and lifestyle. Be prepared to weigh the bad news with the good about the Golden to make a well-informed decision.

SALES CONTRACT

Most reputable breeders have a puppy sales contract that includes specific health guarantees and reasonable return policies. The breeder should agree to accept the puppy back if things do not work out. He also should be willing, indeed anxious, to check up on the puppy's progress after the pup leaves home and be available if you have questions or problems with the pup.

AKC INDEFINITE LISTING PRIVILEGE

Many breeders place their pet-quality puppies on the AKC's Indefinite Listing Privilege (ILP). This does register the pup with AKC and allows the dog to compete in some types of AKC-licensed competition (not conformation), but does not allow AKC registration of any offspring from the mature dog. The purpose of the limited registration is to prevent indis-criminate breeding of "pet-quality" Goldens. The breeder, and only the breeder, can cancel the ILP if the adult dog develops into breeding quality.

REFERENCES

If you have any doubts at all, feel free to ask for references and check with them. It's unlikely that a breeder will offer names of unhappy puppy clients, but calling other owners may make you more comfortable dealing with that particular breeder. Of course, a good reference in itself is that the breeder is a GRCA member. Member breeders can be found listed on the club's website at www.grca.org.

COST

You can expect to pay a dear price for all of these breeder qualities, whether you purchase a "pet-quality" Golden for a companion dog, or one for show or working potential. Good breeders evaluate their puppies, and those with little or no show potential are

CHAPTER 4

considered "pet quality" and sold for less than their "show-quality" pups. While this is completely normal, be aware that a "discount" or "bargain" Golden is not a bargain at all. Indeed, the discount pup is in reality a potential disaster that has little chance of developing into a healthy, stable adult. Such

Watch how all of the breeder's pups interact with the dam. Their affectionate attitude tells you that she's raised them right.

"bargains" could ultimately cost you a fortune in vet expenses, as well as heartache that can't be measured in dollars and cents.

WHERE AND WHERE *NOT* TO LOOK

So how do you find a reputable breeder whom you can trust? Do your homework before you visit puppies. Check with the

American Kennel Club (www.akc.org) and GRCA for breeder referrals in your area. Both of these websites also offer links to regional Golden breed clubs and breeders throughout the United States. Do some research, make some calls and ask about the litters. Any information gleaned from these conversations will make you a smarter shopper when you visit a litter of pups.

Another wonderful opportunity is to spend the day at a dog show or other dog event where you can meet Golden breeders and exhibitors and get to know their dogs. Most Golden devotees are more than happy to show off their dogs and brag about their accomplishments. Further, if you know a Golden of whom you are fond, ask the owner where the dog came from and research the source.

Where *not* to look for your Golden puppy? Skip the puppy ads in your local newspaper. Reputable breeders rarely advertise in newspapers. They don't have to. They are very particular about prospective puppy owners and do not rely on mass advertising to attract the right people. They sell every puppy themselves and never trust anyone to handle their puppy sales (other than a co-breeder friend). Rather, these breeders depend on referrals from their Golden friends and previous puppy clients, and only sell to new owners who pass the puppy "interrogation." A good breeder has an

extended "Golden family." Very often, dedicated breeders will keep puppies past the usual eight-week placement age until the right owners come along.

Perhaps the second most important ingredient in your breeder search is patience. You will not likely find the right breeder or litter on your first go-around. Good breeders often have waiting lists, but a good Golden pup is worth the wait.

SELECTING A BREEDER

Overview

- You are searching for an experienced breeder, uncompromising in ethics and dedicated to the best interests of the breed.
- The litter's pedigrees should show quality ancestors, and the breeder should have good reasons for planning this particular (and every other) mating.
- Be prepared with a list of questions for the breeder; likewise, expect the breeder to interview you so that he is assured of your suitability as an owner.
- Discuss relevant health clearances on the littter's parents. You also should ask to see the appropriate documentation.
- Membership in the GRCA is a good referral on its own. Active involvement in the breed club and breed-related activities further proves a breeder's credibility.

CHAPTER 5

Finding the Right Puppy

Picking the right puppy is the foundation of a happy future with your Golden, and a reputable breeder is a key element in your puppy selection. The breeder's experience with Goldens is invaluable in helping you select your puppy. A good breeder has experience with the Golden, understands the health and genetic issues that affect the breed and selects his breeding stock with care. He also evaluates his puppies and

Surprise! Look who's peeking out to steal your heart!

helps his clients find the pup that will best suit their needs and lifestyle.

You may have to put on your traveling shoes; the perfect puppy is seldom right around the corner. Be willing to travel to visit any litter of pups you are considering and, if possible, visit more than one. You will be surprised at the difference from one litter to the next. You'll be a smarter shopper for your efforts and thus end up with a better pup.

It's obvious that this smiling Golden mom passed her happy, loving nature on to her sweet little one.

A puppy visit involves much more than cuddles and kisses. It's more like your ultimate job interview. While searching for your new Golden family member, you'll be checking out the applicants...the puppies, their parents and the breeder, as well as the living environment in which the pups are raised.

Where and how a litter of pups is raised is vitally important to their early development into confident and social animals. The litter should be

How will you pick your Golden from a peck of precious pups?

CHAPTER 5

kept indoors, in the house or in an adjoining sheltered area, not isolated in a basement, garage or outside kennel building. A few experienced breeders sometimes have separate breeding facilities for their litters. You will know that you have found one of these exceptional breeders when you see the walls lined with blue ribbons and dozens of champion certificates.

Whether kitchen- or kennel-raised, all Golden puppies need to be socialized daily with people and people activities. The greater the pups' exposure to household sights and sounds between three to four weeks of age and eight weeks of age, the easier their adjustment to their future human family.

During your visit, scrutinize the puppies as well as their living area for cleanliness and signs of sickness or poor health. The pups should be reasonably clean (allowing for normal non-stop "puppy-pies"). They should appear energetic, bright-eyed and alert. Healthy pups have clean, thick coats, are well proportioned and feel solid and muscular without being overly fat and pot-bellied. Watch for crusted eyes or noses and any watery discharge from the noses, eyes or ears. Listen for coughing or mucousy sniffing or snorting. Check for evidence of watery or bloody stools.

Visit with the dam and also the sire, if possible. In many cases the sire is not on the premises, but the breeder should have at least photos, his pedigree and a resume of his characteristics and accomplishments. It is normal for some dams to be somewhat protective of their young, but overly aggressive behavior is unacceptable. Golden Retrievers are among the friendliest of creatures, and it's a rare Golden that will shy away from a friendly overture. Temperament is inherited, and if one or both parents are aggressive or very shy, it is likely some of the pups will inherit those atypical and undesirable characteristics.

It's also normal for a new mother to have a rather scrawny coat or be on the thin side after weeks of nursing hungry pups. However, there is an obvious difference between normal post-partum appearance and signs of poor health or neglect.

Notice how the pups interact with their littermates and their surroundings, especially their responses to people. They should be active and outgoing. In most Golden litters, some pups will be more outgoing than others, but even a quiet pup that is properly socialized should not be shy or spooky or shrink from a friendly voice or outstretched hand.

The breeder should be honest in discussing any differences in puppy personalities. Although many breeders do some sort of temperament testing, they also have spent most of their time cuddling and cleaning up after these pups,

and by now know the subtle differences in each pup's personality. The breeder's observations are valuable aids in selecting a Golden puppy

Pups learn much about the ways of dogdom through play and their littermates' reactions to their behavior.

that is right for you, your lifestyle and your goals for the pup.

Tell the breeder if you plan to show your pup in conformation, hunt or compete in sporting activities or Golden-related pursuits. Some pups will show more promise than others, and he can help you select one that will best suit your long-term goals. If you have definite ideas about showing or field trialing, this intention will affect your choice of breeder as well. Show breeders will not sell you a puppy and promise you that he will become your first Field

Champion; likewise, hunting-dog breeders can't promise that the puppy will one day win the Westminster Kennel Club show.

There's also the matter of sex. Do you prefer a male or a female? Which one is right for you? Both sexes are loving and loyal, and the differences are due more to individual personalities than to sex. The adult Golden female is a lovable girl and easy to live with, but she also can be a bit more moody, depending on her whims and hormonal peaks.

The adult male is often up to 2 inches taller than the female and is heavier boned, weighing 65 to 75 pounds. Although males tend to be more even-tempered than bitches, they are also more physical and exuberant during adolescence, which can be problematic in a large and energetic dog. An untrained male can also become dominant with people and other dogs. A solid foundation in obedience is necessary if you want your Golden pup to respect you as his leader.

Intact males tend to be more territorial, especially with other male dogs. Also, in male puppies, both testicles should be descended into the scrotum. A dog with undescended testicles will make a fine pet but will be ineligible to compete in the show ring. The spay/neuter process, advised for all "pet-only" dogs, creates a level playing field and eliminates most of those sex differences. Your Golden will live longer, too.

By the time they are ready to leave the breeder, the pups should have had at least one worming and their first puppy shots, and have vet's certificates verifying their good health at the time of the exam. Some Golden breeders feel that separating the vaccines in a puppy's first shots reduces the possibility of negative reactions to the various components in the combination vaccines. Ask your breeder and your vet for their recommendations about safe inoculations.

The breeder should tell you what the pup has been eating, when and how much. Some send home a small supply of puppy food to mix with your own the first few days. Most breeders also give their clients puppy "take-home" packets, which include a copy of the health certificate, the puppy's pedigree and registration papers, copies of the parents' health clearances and the sales contract if the breeder has one. Many supply literature on the

All lined up, one cuter than the next, but you cannot choose based on looks alone. Under each ball of golden fluff is a unique puppy personality, waiting to find the perfect match.

breed and how to properly raise a Golden Retriever pup. Dedicated breeders know that the more you know, the better the life ahead for their precious Golden pups. Your goal should be to find one of those breeders.

FINDING THE RIGHT PUPPY

Overview

- Visiting several litters provides a quick education in puppy selection. The more you observe, the more you will learn.
- The pups must be raised in clean areas with plenty of opportunity for socialization and contact with humans.
- Look for health and soundness, both physical and temperamental, in the entire litter.
- Meet both parents if possible, as many similarities are passed on.
- Super-active or more mellow? Male or female? Pet, hunting or show dog? The breeder can help guide you to your perfect match, as he knows each individual puppy's personality very well.

Welcoming Your Golden

It's show time—are you sure that you're ready to bring that little fuzzball home? Not to worry. A little advance planning will make your puppy's transition to his new home a safe and happy one. Stock up on your puppy supplies and do a thorough house check to make sure that your home is safe for your puppy (and your house is safe *from* the pup!). Puppy-proof the house *before* your pup comes home. Believe me, you won't have much time once he arrives.

Shopping for puppy supplies is the

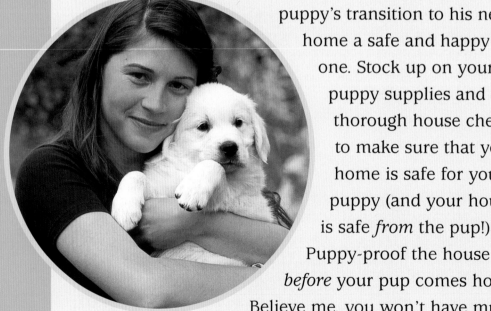

What better way to welcome your new Golden puppy than with lots of love?

fun part, but hang on to your purse strings. Puppy stuff, especially the non-essentials, is often too cute to resist, so "stocking up" can easily decimate your budget. Start with bare essentials, and save the puppy goodies until later.

Select sturdy bowls for your Golden Retriever, made of hard plastic or stainless steel.

FOOD AND WATER BOWLS

You'll need two separate serving pieces, one for food and one for water. Stainless steel pans are your best choice, as they are lightweight, chew-proof and easy to clean. Tip-proof is a good idea, too, since most puppies love to splash about in their water bowls, and the Golden is the epitome of a water-loving pup. You may want an additional water bowl to put outdoors.

This is not what we mean by puppy food! Keep in mind that along with a puppy comes inevitable puppy mischief.

PUPPY FOOD

Your Golden puppy should be fed a quality food that is appropriate for his age and breed. Most quality dog

CHAPTER 6

foods now are offered in breed-specific formulas that address the nutritional needs of small, medium and large (your Golden) breeds of dog during the various stages of their lives. Large-breed puppy food, formulated to promote healthy growth, should be his diet for the first year. After that, you can switch to a large-breed adult-maintenance food.

Your Golden's early growth period as well as his long-term health will benefit from a diet of high-quality puppy and dog food. For experienced recommendations, check with your breeder and your vet before you choose your puppy's food. You may just want to stick with the food that the pup had been fed by the breeder.

COLLARS AND ID TAG
Your Golden pup should have an adjustable collar that expands to fit him as he grows. Lightweight nylon adjustable collars work best for both pups and adult dogs. Put the collar

on as soon as your pup comes home so he can get used to wearing it. The ID tag should have your phone number, name and address, but not the puppy's name, as that would enable a stranger to identify and call your dog. Some owners include a line that says "Dog needs medication" to hopefully speed the dog's return if he is lost or stolen. Attach the tag with an "O" ring (the kind used in key rings), as the more common "S" ring snags on carpets and comes off easily.

Today even dog collars have gone high-tech. Some come equipped with beepers and tracking devices. The most advanced pet identification tool uses a Global Positioning System and fits inside a collar or tag. When your dog leaves his programed home perimeter, the device sends a message directly to your phone or email address.

Choke collars and pinch collars are for training

purposes and should be worn *only* during training sessions. Training collars should never be used on Golden puppies under 16 weeks of age, and do not use a collar that may pull or damage the coat.

LEASHES

For your puppy's safety and your own convenience, his leash wardrobe should include at least two kinds of leads. A narrow six-foot leather or nylon leash is best for walks, puppy kindergarten, other obedience classes and leash training.

The other type of lead is a flexible lead, or "flexi." A flexi is an extendable lead, housed in a large handle, that extends and retracts with the push of a button. This is the ideal tool for exercising puppies and adult dogs and should be a staple for every Golden once he behaves well on a regular lead. Flexis are available in several lengths (8 feet to 26 feet) and strengths, depending on breed size.

Longer is better, as it allows your dog to run about and check out the good sniffing areas farther away from you. They are especially handy for exercising your puppy in unfenced areas or when traveling with your dog.

A sturdy leash and collar with ID tags attached must be staples of every Golden's wardrobe throughout his life.

BEDDING

Dog beds are just plain fun. Beds run the gamut from small and inexpensive to elegant high-end beds suitable for the most royal of dog breeds. However, don't go crazy just yet. Better to save that fancy bed for when your Golden is

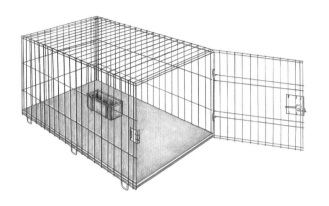

A wire crate provides your Golden puppy with a safe place of his own, makes house-training a quicker and easier process and allows him to feel part of his surroundings while securely confined.

older and less apt to shred it up or make a puddle on it. For puppy bedding, it's best to use a large towel, mat or blanket that can be easily laundered (which will probably be often!).

CRATING AND GATING

These will be your most important puppy purchases. A crate is your most valuable tool for housebreaking your pup and his favorite place to feel secure. Crates come in three varieties: wire mesh, fabric mesh and the familiar plastic airline-type crate. Wire- or fabric-mesh crates offer the best ventilation, and some conveniently fold up suitcase-style. A fabric-mesh crate might

be a little risky for the youngster who likes to dig and chew.

Whatever your choice, purchase an adult-sized crate rather than a small or puppy size; your Golden will soon grow into it. Crates are available at most pet stores and through pet-supply catalogs, and you can figure the adult crate size by adding 6–12 inches to the expected adult height at the withers.

Well-placed sturdy baby gates will protect your house from the inevitable puppy mischief, encouraging good behavior and thus saving your sanity as well. It's wise to confine the puppy to a tiled or uncarpeted room or space, one that is easily cleaned and accessible to the outside door he will use for potty trips. Gated to a safe area where he cannot wreak havoc or destruction, the puppy will soon master Housebreaking 101, chew only appropriate chew toys rather than your antique furniture and spare himself unnecessary corrections for normal puppy mishaps.

Gated, however, does not mean unsupervised. Golden pups bore easily and have been known to entertain themselves by chewing through things like doors and drywall. If your puppy must be unattended, use his crate.

GROOMING TOOLS

Your basic grooming tool should be a soft bristle brush; any kind will do at this young age. Later you will need a slicker brush for routine grooming, a steel comb called a Greyhound comb, which has wide- and narrow-spaced teeth, a mat rake and a shedding comb, the latter two being excellent tools for periods of heavy shedding. Be sure to ask your breeder for suggestions on proper grooming aids.

Introduce your puppy to grooming with a soft bristle brush early on so he learns to like the process. It also helps condition the pup to hands-on attention, which will be invaluable when you have to brush his teeth, clean his ears and clip his nails.

TOYS

Puppies, especially oral breeds like Goldens, love all sorts of fuzzy toys that they can fetch and carry about. Many pups

Introduce your puppy to simple tasks like handling his feet soon after he comes home. This way, he won't be all that surprised when it's time for a pedicure.

will snuggle with their woolly toys as they would their littermates. Eventually most puppies will destroy soft or fuzzy toys, which is your cue to

CHAPTER 6

remove them and no longer buy them.

Of course, retrieving toys are a must for Goldens. Fetching and carrying will be two of his favorite things to do! Safe chew objects are a must if you hope to direct your Golden's chewing onto acceptable objects and away from your shoes and furniture. Hard sterilized bones are

If a Golden pup can reach it, it's going in his mouth. With the ever-mouthy Golden Retriever, you have to be extra-careful about puppy-proofing and keeping potential hazards where the pup cannot get to them.

excellent chewcifiers and come in age-appropriate sizes. Empty gallon milk jugs are all-time favorites, and, best of all, they're free for milk drinkers! They don't last long, though, so discard them as soon as they get scruffy from sharp puppy teeth.

Shoes, socks and slippers are off limits, since even a smart pup can't distinguish his stuff from your own. Also avoid soft, squishy rubber toys or ones with button eyes or squeakers that could be swallowed in a blink. One important puppy toy rule: offer only two or three toys at a time. If you give your puppy a smorgasbord of toys, he will soon become bored with all of them and look for more.

SOCIALIZATION

This actually puppy-proofs your puppy, not your house. Puppy socialization is your Golden's insurance policy to a happy, stable adulthood and is, without question, the most important element in a Golden puppy's introduction to the human world. Although Goldens are by nature outgoing and gregarious dogs, it is still most important to expose them to strangers and new situations at an early age. Canine research has proven that unsocialized pups grow up to be spooky and insecure, and fearful of people, children and strange places. Many turn into fear biters or become aggressive with other dogs, strangers, even family members. Such dogs can seldom be rehabilitated and often end up abandoned in animal shelters, where they unfortunately are ultimately euthanized. Puppy socialization lays the foundation for a well-behaved adult canine, thus preventing destructive and dangerous canine behaviors that lead to these sad scenarios.

A canine's primary socialization period occurs during the puppy's first 20 weeks of life. Once he leaves the safety of his mom and littermates at eight to ten weeks of age, your job begins. Start with a quiet, uncomplicated household for the first day or two, then gradually introduce him to the sights and sounds of his new human world. Frequent interaction with children, new

Puppy Safety at Home

After puppy shopping, you must puppy-proof your house. Golden Retriever pups are naturally curious critters that will investigate everything new, then seek-and-destroy just because it's fun. The message here is: never let your puppy roam your house unsupervised. Scout your house for the following hazards:

Trash Cans and Diaper Pails
These are natural puppy magnets (they know where the good smelly stuff is!)

Medication Bottles, Cleaning Materials, Roach and Rodent Poisons
Lock these up. You'll be amazed at what a determined puppy can find.

Electrical Cords
Unplug wherever you can and make the others inaccessible. Injuries from chewed electrical cords are extremely common in young dogs.

Dental Floss, Yarn, Needles and Thread, and Other Stringy Stuff
Puppies snuffling about at ground level will find and ingest the tiniest of objects and will end up in surgery. Most vets can tell you stories about the stuff they've surgically removed from puppies' guts.

Toilet Bowl Cleaners
If you have them, throw them out now. All dogs are born with "toilet sonar" and quickly discover that the water there is always cold.

Garage
Beware of antifreeze! It is extremely toxic and even a few drops will kill an adult Golden Retriever, less for a pup. Lock it and all other chemicals well out of reach. Fertilizers can also be toxic to dogs.

Socks and Underwear, Shoes and Slippers, Too
Keep them off the floor and close your closet doors. Puppies love all of the above because they smell like you times ten!

CHAPTER 6

people and other dogs is essential at this age. Visit new places (dog-friendly, of course) like parks or even the local grocery-store parking lot where there are crowds of people. Set a goal of two new places a week for the next two months. Keep these new situations upbeat and positive, which will

With all the excitement of coming home to a brand-new place with brand-new people, your Golden will certainly need to take a break.

create a positive attitude toward future encounters.

"Positive" is especially important when visiting your veterinarian. You don't want a pup that quakes with fear every time he sets a paw inside his doctor's office. Make sure your vet is a true dog lover as well as a good dog doctor.

Your puppy also will need supervised exposure to children. Puppies of all breeds tend to view little people like toddlers and small children as littermates and will attempt to exert the upper paw (a dominance ploy) over the child. Because he was bred to hunt and carry game, a Golden pup is very oral and will mouth a child's fingers and toes. Adult family members should supervise and teach the puppy not to nip at or jump up on the kids.

Although Goldens are generally good with children, they are happy, bouncy dogs that could unintentionally overwhelm a small child during play. Both dog and child must be taught how to play properly with each other, and children must learn to handle with care and respect the puppy's privacy. Teach the children not to entice the puppy into rambunctious behavior that could lead to unnecessary corrections.

Take your Golden youngster to puppy school. Some classes accept pups from 10 to 12 weeks of age, with one series of puppy shots as a health requirement. The younger the pup, the easier it is to shape good behavior patterns. A good puppy class teaches proper canine social etiquette rather than rigid obedience skills. Your puppy will meet and play with young dogs of other breeds, and you will learn about the positive teaching tools you'll need to train your pup. Puppy class is important for both novice and experi-enced puppy folks. If you're a smart Golden owner, you won't stop there and will continue on with a basic obedience class. Of course, you want the best-behaved Golden in the neighborhood!

Remember that there is a direct correlation between the quality and amount of time you spend with your puppy during his first 20 weeks of life and the character of the adult dog he will become. You cannot recapture this valuable learning period, so make the most of it.

WELCOMING YOUR GOLDEN

Overview

- Have all of the necessary puppy accessories on hand for your pup's arrival.
- Toys are especially important purchases for the orally fixated Golden.
- Get an adult-sized crate; your puppy will grow into it soon enough.
- Puppy-proofing is essential for keeping both your puppy and your home safe.
- Socialization is fun for a Golden, who lives to make friends, although he needs to be taught to control his natural exuberance so that he doesn't overwhelm his new acquaintances.

Chapter 7

Golden Puppy Kindergarten

Golden Retrievers are smart dogs; after all, isn't that one reason why you chose this breed? They love to learn and are easy to teach, but the key word here is "teach." They are not born pre-programed to be obedient.

Teaching house rules and good manners is your job with your new dog, and this job starts the day you bring your puppy home.

All dogs are pack animals and, as such, they need a leader. Your Golden's first boss was his mother, and all of his life lessons came from his mom and littermates. When he played too rough or nipped too hard, his siblings cried and stopped the

New experiences, like soft strokes with a brush, form the basis of training for future activities. You want a Golden that will behave well during grooming, so it pays to introduce him to it early on.

game. When he got pushy or obnoxious, his mother cuffed him gently with a maternal paw. Now you have to assume the role of leader and communicate appropriate behavior in terms that his young canine mind will understand. Human rules make no sense at all to a dog!

The first 20 weeks of any canine's life are his most valuable learning time. His mind is best able to soak up every lesson, both positive and negative. Positive experiences and proper socialization during this period are critical to his future development and stability. Know this: the amount and quality of time you invest with your Golden youngster now will determine what kind of an adult he will become. Wild dog or gentleman or lady? A well-behaved or naughty dog? It's up to you.

Canine behavioral science tells us that any behavior that is rewarded will be repeated. That's called positive

A smart Golden knows just how to get his way with those who will let him. It's important that all family members play a role in the dog's training and that he's taught to obey everyone with equal respect.

An adorable nine-week-old "sponge," eager to soak up whatever you can teach him.

reinforcement. If something good happens, like a tasty treat or hugs and kisses, a puppy will naturally want to repeat the behavior. That same research also has proven that one of the best ways to a puppy's mind is through his stomach. Never underestimate the power of a treat!

This leads to a very important puppy rule: keep your pockets loaded with puppy treats at all times so you are prepared to reinforce good behavior whenever it occurs. That same reinforcement principle also applies to negative behavior or what we humans might consider negative, like digging in the trash can, which the dog or puppy does not know is "wrong." If the pup gets into the garbage, steals food or does anything else that he thinks is fun or makes him feel good, he will do it again. What better reason to keep a sharp eye on your puppy so you can catch him in the act and teach him

which behaviors are not acceptable to you.

You are about to begin Puppy Class 101. Rule number one: The puppy must learn that you are now the "alpha dog" and his new pack leader. Rule number two: You have to teach him in a manner he will understand (sorry, barking just won't do it.). Remember always that he knows nothing about human standards of behavior.

WORD ASSOCIATION

Use the same word (command) for each behavior every time you teach it, adding food rewards, petting and verbal praise for positive reinforcement. The pup will make the connection and will be motivated to repeat the behavior when he hears those commands. For example, when teaching the pup to potty outside, use the same potty term ("Go potty," "Get busy" and "Hurry up" are commonly used) each time he eliminates, adding a "Good boy!" while he's relieving himself. Your pup will soon learn what those trips outside are for.

TIMING

All dogs learn their lessons in the present tense. You have to catch them in the act (good or bad) in order to dispense rewards or discipline. You have three to five seconds to connect with him or he will not understand what he did wrong. Thus, timing and consistency are your keys to success in teaching any new behavior or correcting bad behaviors.

   Successful puppy training depends on several important principles.

1. Use simple one-word commands and say them only once. Otherwise, puppy learns that "Come" (or "Sit" or "Down") is a three- or four-word command.
2. Never correct your dog for something he did minutes earlier. Three to five seconds, remember?
3. Always praise (and offer a treat) as soon as he does something good (or when he stops doing something naughty). How else will puppy know he's a good dog?
4. Be consistent. You can't

Playing games with your Golden and his toys helps build a bond between the two of you while serving as a precursor to teaching the basic commands.

snuggle together on the couch to watch TV today, then scold him for climbing onto the couch tomorrow.
5. Never tell your dog to come and then correct him for something he did wrong. He will think the correction is for coming to you (think like a dog, remember?). Always go to the dog to stop unwanted behavior, but be sure you catch him in the act or your

dog will not understand the correction.

6. Never hit or kick your dog or strike him with a newspaper or other object. Such physical measures will only create fear and confusion in your dog and could provoke aggressive behavior down the road.

7. When praising or correcting, use your best doggie voice. Use a light and happy voice for praise and a firm, sharp voice for warnings or corrections. A whiny "No, No" or "Drop that" will not sound too convincing, nor will a deep, gruff voice when you say "Good boy" make your puppy feel like having fun.

Your dog also will respond accordingly to family arguments. If there's a shouting match, he will think that he did something wrong and head for cover.

PUPPY GAMES

Puppy games are a great way to entertain your puppy and

yourself, while subliminally teaching lessons in the course of having fun. Start with a game plan and a pocketful of tasty dog treats. Keep your games short so you don't push his attention span beyond normal puppy limits.

"Puppy catch-me" helps teach the come command. With two people sitting on the floor about 10 or 15 feet apart, one person holds and pets the pup while the other calls him: "Puppy, puppy, come!" in a happy voice. When the pup comes running, reward him with big hugs and give a tasty treat. Repeat back and forth several times...don't overdo it.

You can add a ball or toy and toss it back and forth for the puppy to retrieve. When he picks it up, praise and hug some more, give him a goodie to release the toy, then toss it back to person number two. Repeat as described.

Hide and seek is another game that teaches the come exercise. Play this game

Golden Puppy Kindergarten

```

outdoors in your yard or other confined safe area. When the pup is distracted, hide behind a tree or bush. Peek out to see when he discovers you are gone and comes running back to find you (trust me, he will do that). As soon as he gets close, come out, squat down with arms outstretched and call him: "Puppy, come!" This is also an excellent bonding technique and teaches the puppy to depend on you.

Play "Where's your toy?" by placing one of his favorite toys in plain sight, asking your puppy "Where's your toy?" and letting him take it. Repeat several times. Then place your puppy safely outside the room and place the toy where only part of it shows. Bring him back and ask the same question. Praise highly when he finds it. Repeat several times. Finally, conceal the toy completely and let your puppy sniff it out. Trust his nose…he will find his toy.

Golden puppies love to have fun with their people. Games are excellent teaching aids, and one of the best ways to say "I love you" to your puppy.

## GOLDEN PUPPY KINDERGARTEN

### Overview

- The Golden is intelligent, but he is not born trained! Your puppy will be very capable of learning what you teach him.
- You must take advantage of your pup's youth, as this is the time to establish your leadership and his good habits.
- Training methods should be based on positive reinforcement with rewards of treats, petting and praise.
- Teaching word association and knowing how to use correct timing are two basic principles of training.
- Playing games with your puppy will reinforce your bond with each other and introduce commands in a fun way.
```

House-training Your Golden

L et's call this chapter "Crate-training" instead. A dog crate (which is *not* a cage!) is really just a dog den of sorts, a place to keep your puppy safe and out of mischief and to keep your house safe from your puppy. This is perhaps the most important piece of dog equipment you will buy, your Golden's special place all his own that both of you will appreciate and enjoy. Because all canines are natural den creatures, thanks to the thousands of years their ancestors spent living in caves and cavities in the ground, your puppy will adapt quite naturally to crate confinement. Your

House-training is the key to a happy life with a clean companion with whom it's a joy to share your home.

Golden puppy is an inherently clean little fellow, and he will try hard not to soil his personal living space.

The crate is actually a multi-purpose dog accessory: your Golden's personal dog house within your house, a humane house-training tool, a security measure that will protect your puppy, home and belongings when you're not home, a travel aid to house and protect your dog when you are traveling (most motels will accept a crated dog) and, finally, a comfy dog space for your puppy when your anti-dog relatives come to visit.

Crate-training a dog in the home means he will be amenable to spending time in the crate whenever the need arises, such as during travel, at dog shows, at the vet's office, etc.

Some experienced breeders insist on crate use after their puppies leave, and a few even begin crate-training their pups before they send them home. But it's more likely that your pup has never seen a crate, so it's up to you to make sure his introduction to the crate is a pleasant one.

Introduce the crate as soon as pup comes home so he learns that this is

For an owner without a yard to accommodate her dog's bathroom needs, a regular schedule of walks for potty purposes must be part of the daily routine.

his new "house." This is best accomplished with dog treats. For the first day or two, toss a tiny treat into the crate to entice him to go in. Pick a crate command, such as "Kennel," "Inside" or "Crate," and use it every time he enters. You also can feed his first few meals inside the crate with the door still open, so the crate association will be a happy one.

Your puppy should sleep in his crate from his very first night. He may whine at first and object to the confine-ment, but be strong and stay the course. If you release him when he cries, you provide his first life lesson…if I cry, I get out and maybe hugged. A better scheme is to place the crate next to your bed at night for the first few weeks. Your presence will comfort him, and you'll also know if he needs a midnight potty trip. Whatever you do, do not lend comfort by taking the puppy into bed with you. To a dog,

on the bed means equal, which is not a good idea this early in the game when you are trying to establish leadership.

Make a practice of placing your puppy in his crate for naps, at nighttime and whenever you are unable to watch him closely. Not to worry…he will let you know when he wakes up and needs a potty trip. If he falls asleep under the table and wakes up when you're not there, guess what he'll do first? Make a puddle, then toddle over to say "Hi!"

Become a Golden vigilante. Routines, consis-tency and an eagle eye are your keys to house-training success. Puppies always "go" when they wake up (quickly now!), within a few minutes after eating, after play periods and after brief periods of confinement. Most pups under 12 weeks of age will need to eliminate at least every hour or so, which can mean 10 or more times a day! (Set your oven timer to remind you.) Always take the puppy outside to the same area, telling him "Outside" as you go out. Pick a "potty" word ("Hurry up," "Go potty" and "Get busy" are the most commonly used), and use it when he does his business, giving him "Good puppy!" praise, repeating your key word. Use the same exit door for these potty trips, and confine puppy to the exit area so he can find it when he needs it. Watch for sniffing and circling or other signs signaling that he has to relieve himself. Don't allow him to roam the house until he's house-trained; how will he find that outside door if he's three or four rooms away? He does not have a house map in his head.

Of course he will have accidents. All puppies do. If you catch him in the act, clap your hands loudly and say "Aaah! Aaah!" and scoop him up to go outside. Your voice should startle him and make him stop. Be sure to praise when he finishes his duty outside.

If you discover the piddle spot after the fact...more than three or four seconds

We all know "what goes in must come out." What puppy owners must know is "what goes in must come out quickly!"

later...you're too late. Pups only understand *in the moment*, and will not understand a correction given more than five seconds (that's only *five*) after the deed. Correcting any later will only cause fear and confusion. Just forget it and vow to be more vigilant.

Never (that is spelled *n-e-v-e-r*) rub your puppy's nose in his mistake or strike your puppy or adult dog with your hand, a newspaper or other object to correct him. He will not understand and will only become fearful of the person who is hitting him.

House-training hint: remove the puppy's water after 7 p.m. to aid in nighttime bladder control. If he gets thirsty, offer him an ice cube. Then just watch him race for the refrigerator when he hears the rattle of the ice-cube tray.

Despite its many benefits, crate use can be abused. Puppies under 12 weeks of age should never be confined for more than two hours at a time, unless, of course, they are sleeping. A general rule of thumb is three hours maximum for a three-month-old pup, four to five hours for the four- to five-month-old, and no more than six hours for dogs over six months of age. If you're unable to be home to release the dog, arrange for a relative, neighbor or dog sitter to let him out to exercise and potty.

One final, but most important, rule of crate use: never, *ever*, use the crate for punishment. Successful crate use depends on your puppy's positive association with his "house." If the crate represents punishment or "bad dog stuff," he will resist using it as his safe place. Sure, you can crate your pup after he has sorted through the trash so you can clean up. Just don't do it in an angry fashion or tell him "Bad dog, crate!"

If you are crate-shy, what can you do with your uncrated puppy when you're not home? Confine him to one room with baby gates or other dog-proof barrier.

Puppy-proof the room by removing anything pup could chew or damage and hurt himself in the process. But even in a stripped environment, some pups will chew through drywall. An exercise pen 4 feet by 4 feet square (available through pet suppliers) sturdy enough that pup can't knock it down, will provide safe containment for short periods. Paper one area for elimination, with perhaps a blanket in the opposite corner for napping. Safe chew toys should help keep him happy while you're gone.

Most importantly, remember that successful house-training revolves around consistency and repetition. Maintain a strict schedule and use your key words consistently. Well-trained owners have well-trained pups...and clean, nice-smelling houses!

HOUSE-TRAINING YOUR GOLDEN

Overview

- Crate-training is the most reliable method of house-training. The crate offers additional benefits of keeping the dog safe in the home and during travel, and in any situation when you can't be there to supervise.
- The pup should associate his crate only with positive things so that he learns to accept it as his den, his very own safe place.
- Be vigilant in taking your pup out to relieve himself often. Prevention is the best way to avoid accidents indoors.
- Praise your pup when he goes in the proper place and only scold him for an accident if you catch him in the act. The reprimand will do no good otherwise—remember your timing!
- Learn how to use a crate properly; never over-use it or use it as a form of punishment.

Teaching Basic Commands

Golden Retrievers are among the smartest of canines. The author has had the pleasure of training dozens of Goldens over the years (most of whom were her own house dogs), and every single Golden has been a joy (and sometimes a challenge) to train into becoming an exceptionally obedient and well-mannered canine companion. Good canine behavior is more than just good house manners. All dogs should learn basic obedience if they are to be welcome wherever they go. They should be proficient in simple commands such as come, sit, stay,

In order to begin teaching commands, your Golden pup must be accustomed to his collar and lead.

down and heel. Flawless, in fact.

You can start your puppy's lessons as soon he comes home. Don't worry, he's not too young. This is his prime learning period, so the earlier you start, the easier the process and the more successful you both will be. Always start your teaching exercises in a quiet, distraction-free environment. Once your Golden pup has mastered any task, change the setting and practice in a different location...another room, the yard, then with another person or a dog nearby. If the pup reacts to the new distraction and does not perform the exercise, back up and continue with the exercise by removing the distractions for a while. Don't rush things. Remember that he's just a pup!

Appoint one person to instruct your puppy in the early stages to avoid confusing the pup. Once your puppy has learned a command reliably, other family members can join in.

The sit position is the first you will teach. It is the easiest to learn, and it forms the basis for other commands, such as heel, in which the dog starts out sitting by your side until you start to walk.

To begin teaching your Golden to stay, start with him in the sit position and your hand near his nose as a "stop sign."

CHAPTER 9

Ignore your Golden puppy for a few minutes before each training session. The lack of stimulation will make him more eager for your company and attention. Keep sessions short so your puppy won't get bored or lose his enthusiasm. In time, he will be able to

For those with aspirations to show, the Golden must be taught to stay in the standing (or "stacked") position, which he will assume for evaluation in the ring. Many handlers teach this exercise by focusing the dog's attention on a treat.

concentrate for longer periods. Vary the exercises to keep his enthusiasm level high. Watch for signs of boredom and loss of attention.

Always keep your training sessions positive and upbeat. Use lots of praise, praise and more praise! Never train your puppy or adult dog if you are in a grumpy mood. You will lose patience, and he will think it is his fault. That will reverse any progress the two of you have made. Finish every training session on a positive note. If you have been struggling or unsuccessful, switch gears and do something he knows well (like sit!) and end the session.

Before you can effectively teach your puppy any command, two things must happen. Puppy must learn to respond to his name (name recognition), and you must be able to gain and hold his attention. How to accomplish that? Why, with treats, of course! Treats are defined as tiny tidbits, preferably soft easy-to-chew treats. We don't want to overfeed this pup. Thin slices of hot dogs cut in quarters work well.

ATTENTION AND NAME RECOGNITION

Start by calling your Golden puppy's name. Once. Not two or three times, but once. Otherwise, he will learn he has a three-part name and will ignore you when you say it once. Begin by using his name when he is undistracted and you are sure he will look at you, and pop him a treat as soon as he does so. Repeat about a dozen times, several times a day. It won't take more than a day or so before he understands that his name means something good to eat.

RELEASE COMMAND

That's the word you'll use to tell him the exercise is over, similar to "At ease" in the military. "All done" and "Free" are the ones most commonly recommended; "Okay" is also used. You'll need this release word so your Golden will know that the exercise is over and it's okay to relax and/or move from a stationary position.

TAKE IT AND LEAVE IT

These commands offer too many advantages to list. Place a treat in the palm of your hand and tell your puppy to "Take it" as he grabs the treat. Repeat three times. On the fourth time, do not say a word as your dog reaches for the treat…just close your fingers around the treat and wait. Do not pull away, but be prepared for the pup to paw, lick, bark and nibble on your fingers. Patience! When he finally pulls away from your hand and waits for a few seconds, open your hand and tell him "Take it." Repeat until he pauses and waits for your command to "Take it."

Now the next step. Show your Golden the treat in the palm of your hand and tell him to "Leave it." When he goes for the treat, close your hand and repeat "Leave it." Repeat the process until he pulls away, wait just a second, then open your hand, tell him to "Take it" and allow him to take the treat.

Repeat the "Leave it" process until he waits just a few seconds, then give the treat on "Take it." Gradually extend the time you wait after your puppy "Leaves it" and before you tell him to "Take it."

Now you want to teach your Golden to leave things on the ground, not just in your hand. (Think of all the things you don't want him to pick up.) With your puppy on a loose leash, position yourself in front of him and toss a treat behind you and a little to the side so he can see it, while saying "Leave it." Here begins the dance. If he goes for the treat, use your body, not your hands, to block him, moving him backwards away from it. As soon as he backs off and gives up trying to get around you, unblock the treat and tell him "Take it." Be ready to block again if he goes for it before you give permission. Repeat the process until he understands and waits for the command.

Once your Golden knows this well, practice with his food dish, telling him to "Leave it," then "Take it" after he complies (he can either sit or stand while waiting for his dish). As before, gradually extend the waiting period before you tell him "Take it."

This little training exercise sends many messages to your Golden. He is reminded that you're the boss and in control and that all good things, like food, come from the human who loves him. It will help prevent your puppy from becoming too possessive of his food bowl, a behavior that only escalates and leads to more serious aggressive behaviors. The benefits of a solid Take it/Leave it are endless.

COME COMMAND
This command has life-saving potential, preventing your Golden from running after a squirrel, chasing a child on a bike, darting into the street…and possible disaster.

Always practice the come command on leash and in a safely confined area. You can't afford to risk failure or the pup will learn he does not have to come when called.

Once you have the pup's attention, call him from a short distance: "Puppy, come!" (use your happy voice) and give a treat when he comes to you. If he hesitates, tug him to you gently with his leash. Grasp and hold his collar with one hand as you dispense the treat. The collar grasp is important. You will eventually phase out the treat and switch to hands-on praise. This maneuver also connects holding his collar with coming and treating, which will assist you in countless future behaviors.

Do 10 or 12 repetitions 2 or 3 times a day. Once your pup has mastered come, continue to practice daily to imprint this most important behavior onto his brain. Experienced Golden owners know, however, that one can never completely trust

a dog to come when called if the dog is on bent on a self-appointed mission. Off leash is often synonymous with out of control. Always keep your Golden on a leash when not in a securely enclosed place.

SIT COMMAND

This one's a snap, since your Golden already understands the treating process. Stand in front of your pup, move the treat directly over his nose and slowly move it backwards over his head. As he folds backwards to reach the goodie, his rear will move downward to the floor. If the puppy raises up to reach the treat, just lower it a bit. The moment his

You want your Golden always to respond reliably when you call him to come to you. More often than not, he will come running to show you what he's carrying around at the moment (in which case "Leave it" might prove handy!).

behind is down, tell him "Sit." That's one word, "Sit." Release the treat and gently grasp the collar as you did with the come. He will again make that positive connection between the treat, the sit position and the collar hold.

As he becomes more proficient, make him hold the sit position longer before you give the treat (this is the beginning of the stay command). Begin

Once your Golden has mastered the down, which could prove a challenge, you can progress to teaching him to stay in that position as you did with the sit.

using your release word to release him from the sit position. Practice using the sit command for everyday activities like sitting for his food bowl or a toy, and do random sits throughout the day, always

for a food or praise reward. Once he is reliable, combine the "Sit" and "Leave it" for his food dish. Your Golden is expanding his vocabulary.

STAY COMMAND

"Stay" is really just an extension of "Sit," which your Golden already knows. With puppy sitting when commanded, place the palm of your hand in front of his nose and tell him "Stay." Count to five. Give him his release word to end the stay and praise. Stretch out the stays in tiny increments, making allowances for puppy energy.

Once he stays reliably, move your body a step backwards after giving the command, then step forward again. Gradually extend the time and distance that you move away. If puppy moves, say "No" and move in front of him. Use sensible timelines, depending on your puppy's attention span.

DOWN COMMAND

Down can be a tough command to master. Because down is a submissive posture, some dogs and certain take-charge breeds may find it especially difficult. That's why it's most important to teach it when they're very young.

From the sit position, move the food lure from his nose to the ground and slightly backwards between his front paws. Wiggle it as necessary to spark his interest. As soon as his front legs and rear end hit the floor, give the treat and tell him "Down, good boy, down!" thus connecting the word to the behavior. "Down" may prove difficult, so be patient and generous with the praise when he cooperates. Once he goes into the down position with ease, incorporate the stay as you did with sit. By six months of age, your puppy should be able to do a 10-minute solid sit/stay, ditto for a down/stay.

WAIT COMMAND

You'll love this one, especially when your Golden comes into the house with wet or muddy paws. Work on the wait command with a closed interior door. (It would not be wise to try this with an outside exit door.) Start to open the door as if to go through or out. When your dog tries to follow, step in front and body-block him to prevent his passage. Don't use the wait command just yet. Keep blocking until he hesitates and you can open the door a little to pass through. Then say your wait release word, "Through" or "Okay" or whatever release word you have chosen for this exercise, and let him go through the door. Repeat by body-blocking until he understands and waits for you, then start applying the actual word "Wait" to the behavior. Practice in different doorways, using outside entrances (to safely enclosed areas only) once he will wait reliably.

HEEL COMMAND

The formal heel command comes a bit later. A young Golden should be taught simply to walk politely on a leash, at or near your side. That is best accomplished when your pup is very young and small, before he can pull you down the street!

Your Golden will revel in the opportunity to explore an open field on a long lead, but he must also heel politely by your side when you want him to.

Start leash training soon after your pup comes home. Simply attach his leash to his buckle collar and let him drag it around for a little while every day. Play a puppy game with the leash on. Make wearing his leash a happy moment in his day. If he chews the leash, distract him with a play activity. You also can spray the leash with a product sold at the pet shop designed to make it taste unpleasant to discourage chewing.

After a few days, gather up the leash in a distraction-free zone of the house or yard and take just a few steps together. With your puppy on your left side, hold a treat lure at his eye level to encourage him to walk next to you. Pat your knee and use a happy voice. Use the phrase "Let's go!" as you move forward, holding the treat low to keep him near. Take a few steps, give the treat and praise. Move forward just a few steps each time.

Keep these sessions short and happy, a mere 30 seconds at a time (that's long in puppy time). Never scold or nag him into walking faster or slower, just encourage him with happy talk. Walk straight ahead at first, adding wide turns once he gets the hang of it. Progress to 90° turns, using a gentle leash tug on the turns, a happy verbal "Let's go!" and, of course, a treat. Walk in short 10- to 20-second bursts with happy breaks (use your release word) and brief play in between. Keep total training time short and always quit with success, even if just a few short steps.

KEEP PRACTICING

Ongoing practice is actually a lifetime dog rule, especially for a strong-willed dog. Dogs will be dogs, and if we don't maintain their skills, they will sink back into sloppy, inattentive behaviors that will be harder to correct. Incorporate these commands into your daily routine and your Golden will remain a gentleman or lady of whom you can be proud.

TEACHING BASIC COMMANDS

Overview

- All dogs need an education in the basic commands. Fortunately, the Golden is very intelligent and very trainable.
- The Golden is a friendly and loving dog who should never receive harsh treatment. Positive reinforcement is the way to go in teaching your dog.
- Start by choosing an appropriate name and teaching your dog to recognize it. You must be able to get his attention before training begins.
- Pick a release word to use with each command to signify that the exercise is over.
- The basic commands include take it/leave it, sit, stay, down, heel, come and wait. Keep practicing and incorporate these exercises into your everyday routine.

Home Care for Your Golden

The average Golden Retriever lives, on average, 10 to 13 years. The quality of those years depends on a conscientious home health-care program. Although genetics and the environment certainly influence a dog's longevity, the fact remains that you are the backbone of your Golden's health-maintenance program. Like the proverbial apple a day, your daily focus on canine wellness will help "keep the veterinarian away."

The two most important health regimens are, without a moment's doubt, weight control and dental hygiene. Veterinarians tell us that over

Your good care at home means a Golden who will be healthier and happier, for longer!

50% of the dogs they see are grossly overweight, and that such obesity will take two to three years off a dog's life, given the strain it puts on the animal's heart, lungs and joints. The obvious message here: lean is healthier, and those are words to live by for chow-hound owners.

In addition to contributing to healthy weight maintenance, good nutrition plays a big role in coat condition. A healthy diet will shine through in the Golden's lustrous locks.

WEIGHT CONTROL

If your Golden could suddenly speak, the first thing that he would say is, "Who are you calling a chow-hound?" No Golden has ever been accused of having a poor appetite! To determine if your Golden is overweight, you should be able to feel your dog's ribs beneath a thin layer of muscle with very gentle pressure on his rib cage. When viewing your dog from above, you should be able to see a definite waistline; from the side, he should have an obvious tuck-up in his abdomen.

Safe chews also have dental benefits. Sturdy rope toys act like floss as the dog chews, getting between teeth to remove hard-to-reach particles and tartar.

Keep a record of his weight from

each annual vet visit. A few extra pounds? Adjust his food portions (and no table scraps), perhaps switch to a "light," "senior" or lower-calorie dog food formula and increase his exercise.

Excessive weight is especially hard on older dogs with creaky joints. A senior Golden who is sedentary will grow out of shape more quickly. Walking and running (slower for old guys) are still the best workouts for health maintenance. Tailor your dog's exercise to fit his age and physical condition.

ORAL HYGIENE
Now that your dog is slim and trim, let's examine his teeth. The American Veterinary Dental Society states that 80% of dogs show signs of oral disease as early as age three. Further studies prove that good oral hygiene can add three to five years to a dog's life. (Quick, look at your dog's teeth!)

Danger signs include yellow and brown build-up of tartar along the gumline, red, inflamed gums and persistent bad breath. If neglected, these conditions will allow bacteria to accumulate in your dog's mouth and enter your dog's bloodstream through those damaged gums, increasing the risk for disease in vital organs such as the heart, liver and kidneys. It is known that periodontal disease is a major contributor to kidney disease, which is a common cause of death in older dogs...and highly preventable.

Your vet should examine your Golden's teeth and gums during his annual checkups to make sure they are clean and healthy. He may recommend professional cleaning if there is excessive plaque build-up.

During the other 364 days a year, you are your dog's dentist. Brush his teeth daily, or at least twice a week. Use a doggie toothbrush (designed for the contour of a canine's mouth) and use dog toothpaste flavored with chicken, beef and liver. (Minty people paste is harmful to dogs.) If your dog resists a toothbrush, try a nappy washcloth or gauze pad

carrot every day. Carrots help scrub away plaque while providing extra vitamins A and C. Invest in healthy chew objects, such as nylon or rubber

Given the choice, your Golden would gladly accompany you every-where you go! Part of responsible dog care is ensuring his safety and comfort during travel, whether to the vet or on vacation.

wrapped around your finger. Start the brushing process with gentle gum massages when your Golden is very young so he will learn to tolerate and even enjoy the process.

Feeding dry dog food is an excellent way to help minimize plaque accumulation. You can also treat your dog to a raw

bones and toys with ridges that act as tartar scrapers. There are special dental-care bones designed to help remove and prevent plaque. Raw beef knuckle bones (cooked bones will splinter) also work, but watch for sharp edges and splintering on these or any chew object, which can cut the dog's mouth and intestinal lining if swallowed. Rawhides do not digest easily and can cause choking if the dog swallows large chunks, as many dogs tend to do. If you offer rawhides, do so infrequently and only under supervision.

CHECKING OVER THE COAT

Your weekly grooming sessions should include body checks for lumps (cysts, warts and fatty

Not all flowers are as pretty as they look. Many can be toxic to dogs or cause allergic reactions. Acquaint yourself with these troublesome plants before your pup comes home to ensure that none are kept in your home or yard where puppy may roam.

tumors), hot spots and other skin or coat problems. While harmless skin lumps are common in older dogs, many can be malignant, and your vet should examine any abnormality. Black mole-like patches or growths on any body part require immediate veterinary inspection. Remember, petting and hugging can also turn up little abnormalities.

Be extra-conscious of dry skin, a flaky coat and thinning hair, all signs of possible thyroid disease. Check for fleas and flea dirt (especially on your dog's underside and around the base of the tail) if you think fleas could be present.

EAR CARE

Check your dog's ears weekly…are they clean and fresh-smelling? Have your vet show you the proper way to clean them. Remember too, many old dogs grow deaf with age. Sure, a smart dog develops selective hearing and sometimes will not "hear" you, but you'll know it's a true hearing deficit when your Golden no longer hears the clinking of the cookie jar. Time and experience will show you what changes and allowances to make if your dog develops hearing loss.

EYE CARE

Your Golden's vision may deteriorate with age. A bluish haze is common in geriatric dogs and does not impair vision. But you should always check with your vet about any changes in the eyes to determine if they are harmless or indicative of a problem.

UNDER THE HOOD

How about his other end… does he chew at his rear or scoot and rub it on the carpet? That's a sign of impacted anal glands. Have your vet express those glands. (It's not a job for amateurs.) Do annual stool cultures to check for intestinal parasites; hook-, whip- and roundworms can cause weight and appetite loss, poor coat quality and all manner of intestinal problems, which can weaken your dog's resistance to other canine diseases. See your vet if any of those signs appear. Tapeworms, another common parasite, which come from fleas, look like grains of rice tucked in the stool.

HEART DISEASE

Heart disease is common in all canines, yet it is one that dog owners most frequently overlook. Symptoms include panting and shortness of breath, chronic coughing, especially at night or upon first waking in the morning, and changes in sleeping habits. Heart disease can be treated if you catch it early.

KIDNEY DISEASE

Kidney disease also can be treated successfully with early diagnosis. Dogs seven years and older should be tested annually for kidney and liver function. If your dog drinks excessive amounts of water, urinates more frequently and/or has accidents in the house, run, don't walk, to your vet. Kidney disease can be managed with

CHAPTER 10

special diets to reduce the workload on the kidneys.

DOGGY EMERGENCIES

For everyday commonsense care, every dog owner should know the signs of an emergency. Many dog agencies, humane societies and animal shelters sponsor canine first-aid seminars. Participants learn

Active dogs like the Golden play hard and rest hard! This is normal, but being sluggish, lethargic or uninterested in activity is not. Alert the vet if you notice any of these out-of-the-ordinary symptoms in your dog.

how to recognize and deal with signs of common emergency situations, how to assemble a first aid kit, how to give CPR to a dog and more. The moral here is: know your Golden. Early detection of any problem is the key to your dog's longevity and quality of life.

Signs of an emergency include vomiting for more than 24 hours, bloody or prolonged (over 24 hours) diarrhea, fever (normal canine temperature is 101.5°F) and a sudden swelling of the head or any body part (allergic reaction to an insect bite or other stimulus).

Some symptoms of other more common emergency situations include:

Heatstroke: Excessive panting, drooling, rapid pulse, dark reddened gums and a frantic, glazed expression (you'll know it when you see it.)

Hypothermia (wet dogs + cold weather): Shivering, very pale gums and body temperature under 100°F.

Shock: Severe blood loss from an injury can send a dog into shock. Symptoms include shivering, weak pulse, weakness and listlessness, depression and lowered body temperature.

Additional red flags for cancer or other serious health problems include: lumps or abnormal swelling; sores that do not heal; sudden or unexplainable weight loss; loss of appetite; unexplained bleeding or discharge; an offensive body odor; difficulty swallowing or eating; loss of stamina or reluctance to exercise; difficulty breathing, urinating or defecating; a bloated appearance; persistent stiffness or lameness.

Call your vet at once if you notice any of these warning signs. Many canine diseases and some cancers are treatable if they are diagnosed in the early stages.

Cultivate a keen awareness of even subtle changes in your dog. Read books on canine health care and first aid and add one to your library. Keep a list of symptoms and remedies in a handy place to reference when necessary; also have your first-aid kit and your vet's emergency phone number in a convenient place. Your Golden's life could depend on it.

HOME CARE FOR YOUR GOLDEN

Overview

- You are responsible for your dog's health. His longevity and overall quality of life depend much on the care he receives at home.
- Keeping your Golden at a proper weight is essential. Obesity is very detrimental to a dog, and your Golden certainly won't put himself on a diet!
- In between visits to the vet, you are your dog's dentist, too.
- Thoroughly check your Golden's abundant coat, all the way down to the skin, to make sure all looks and feels normal and healthy.
- Regularly check the ears, eyes and anal glands, and know the signs of internal problems like heart and kidney disease.
- Acquaint yourself with canine first-aid techniques and the signs of emergencies.

Feeding Your Golden Retriever

Few dog issues are more confusing...or more critical...than food. Your Golden should have a quality food that is appropriate for his age and lifestyle. Only a premium quality food will provide the proper balance of the vitamins, minerals and fatty acids that are necessary to support healthy bone, muscle, skin and coat. The major dog-food manufacturers have developed their formulas with strict quality controls, using only quality ingredients obtained from reliable sources. The labels on the food bags tell you what products are in the food (beef,

"You are what you eat" holds true for dogs, too. Do some research and ask advice of experienced dog folk to help you determine the best diet for your Golden at his particular stage of life.

chicken, corn, etc), and list ingredients in descending order of weight or amount in the food. Do not add your own supplements, "people food" or extra vitamins to the food. You will only upset the nutritional balance of the food, which could affect the growth pattern or maintenance of your Golden.

Mealtime means good-behavior time! There are many ways to reinforce your dog's knowledge of the basic commands as part of your everyday routine, such as sitting politely for his food bowl.

The premium dog-food brands now offer foods for every breed size, age and activity level. As with human infants, puppies require a diet different from that of an adult canine. New growth formulas contain protein and fat levels that are appropriate for the different-sized breeds. Large-breed, fast-growing dogs (your Golden) require less protein and fat during these early months of rapid growth, which is better for healthy joint development. Medium and small breeds have different nutritional requirements during their first year of growth.

You want your Golden to be part of all you do, but you have to draw the line somewhere. Your Golden should not be fed from the table, as this encourages begging; "people food" treats should be avoided as a matter of course anyway.

In the world of quality dog foods, there are enough choices to befuddle even experienced dog folks. Don't be intimidated by all those dog-food bags on the store shelves. Read the labels on the bags (how else can you learn what's in those foods?) and call the information number on the dog-food bag. Ask your breeder and your vet what

There are many types of food and water bowls available. Ask your vet if it is beneficial or not to provide your Golden with elevated bowls.

food they recommend for your Golden pup. A solid education in the dog-food business will provide the tools you need to offer your dog a diet that is best for his long-term health. If you plan to switch from the food fed by your breeder, take home a small supply of the breeder's food to mix with your own to

aid your puppy's adjustment to his new food.

An eight-week-old puppy does best eating three times a day. At about 12 weeks of age, you can switch to twice-daily feeding. Most breeders suggest two meals a day for the life of the dog, for better digestion and bloat prevention. Free-feeding, that is, leaving a bowl of food available all day, is not recommended. Free-feeding fosters picky eating habits…a bite here, a nibble there. Free-feeders are also more likely to become possessive of their food bowls, a problem behavior that signals the beginning of aggression. Scheduled meals also give you one more opportunity to remind your Golden that all good things in life come from you, his owner and chef.

With scheduled meals, it's also easier to predict elimination, which is the better road to house-training. Regular meals help you know just how much your puppy eats and when, which is valuable information for weight control and recognizing changes in appetite.

Should you feed canned or dry food, offer the dry food with or without water? Dry food is recommended by most vets, since the dry particles help clean the dog's teeth of plaque and tartar. Adding water to dry food is optional. The food hog who almost inhales his food will do better with a splash of water in his food pan. A bit of water added immediately before eating is also thought to enhance the flavor of the food, while still preserving the dental benefits. Whether feeding wet or dry, have water available at all times, although limiting water at mealtimes is a bloat preventative.

Like people, puppies and adult dogs have different appetites; some will lick their food bowls clean and beg for more, while others pick at their food and leave some of it

BLOAT IN THE GOLDEN RETRIEVER

Deep-chested breeds are prone to the deadly condition known as bloat, caused by rapid accumulation of air and the subsequent rotation of the stomach. The Golden Retriever is at risk, so owners should take precautions to protect their dogs from the possible onset of bloat. Here are some commonsense steps to avoid your dog's swallowing air while he's eating and to prevent upsetting his digestion:

- Buy top-quality dog food that is high nutrition/low residue. Test a kibble in a glass of water. If it swells up to four times its original size, try another brand.

- No vigorous exercise for at least one hour before and two hours after all meals.

- Never allow your dog to gulp his food or water. Feed him when he is calm.

- Place large unswallowable objects in his bowl to prevent him from "inhaling" his food in two mouthfuls.

- Add small amounts of canned food to the dry.

Discuss further preventatives and the symptoms of bloat with your vet, as *immediate* treatment is necessary to save an affected dog's life.

untouched. It's easy to overfeed a chow-hound. Who can resist those soulful Golden eyes? Be strong and stay the right course. Chubby puppies may be cute and cuddly, but the extra weight will stress their growing joints and is thought to be a factor in the development of hip and elbow disease. Overweight pups also tend to grow into overweight adults who tire easily and will be more susceptible to other health problems. Consult your breeder and your vet for advice on how to adjust meal portions as your puppy grows.

So always remember that

lean is healthy, fat is not. Research has proven that obesity is a major canine killer. Quite simply, a lean dog lives longer than one who is overweight. And that doesn't even reflect the better quality of life for the lean dog that can run, jump and play without the burden of an extra 10 or 20 pounds. As a rule, avoid feeding table scraps. You don't want to encourage begging; plus, some "people foods" like chocolate, onions, grapes, raisins and certain nuts are toxic to dogs.

If your adult Golden is overweight, you can switch to a "light" food which has fewer calories and more fiber. "Senior" foods for older dogs have formulas designed to meet the needs of less active, older dogs. "Performance" diets contain more fat and protein for dogs that compete in sporting disciplines or lead very active lives.

To further complicate the dog-food dilemma, there are

Now this is restraint! You know you have a well-trained dog when he can behave politely around food!

Feeding Your Golden Retriever

also raw foods available for those who prefer to feed their dogs a completely natural diet rather than traditional manufactured dog food. The debate on raw and/or all-natural vs. manufactured dog food is a fierce one, with some raw proponents claiming that raw diets have cured their dogs' allergies and other chronic ailments. If you are interested in this alternative feeding method, check out books written by canine nutrition experts on this type of feeding method. You also can check with your vet, ask your breeder and surf the Internet.

The bottom line is this: What and how much you feed your Golden is a major factor in his overall health and longevity. It's worth your investment in extra time and dollars to provide the best diet for your dog.

FEEDING YOUR GOLDEN RETRIEVER

Overview

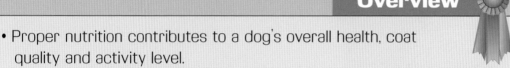

- Proper nutrition contributes to a dog's overall health, coat quality and activity level.
- Your Golden pup should be fed a high-quality puppy food formulated to promote healthy growth in large-breed puppies.
- Once your Golden reaches adulthood, he will need a quality large-breed maintenance formula, keeping in mind that very active dogs have different nutritional requirements from those that get less exercise.
- The frequency of feedings will decrease as the puppy grows. A morning and evening schedule is good for an adult Golden.
- Scheduled feedings help you know your dog's appetite and thus detect any changes.
- Don't attempt an alternative feeding method without a solid education in canine nutrition!

Grooming Your Golden Retriever

I f you own a Golden Retriever, grooming will be your middle name. You will need a structured grooming program to keep your Golden's coat healthy and neat-looking and to minimize those clouds of wispy golden hair on your furniture and clothing.

Good grooming habits, established early in your Golden's life, are as important to his physical well-being as exercise and diet. Grooming should be a weekly process all year long. Besides caring for the coat, skin, ears, teeth and nails, grooming is a safety check for lumps, bumps, hot

A rich gold coat and a jaunty red bandana— now that's a handsome Golden!

spots and other abnormalities that can hide beneath your dog's fur coat. It will also uncover any tiny critters, like fleas or ticks, which may have sneaked aboard your dog. And let's not forget the bonding benefits of hands-on attention.

Every dog should enjoy the hands-on grooming process; after all, it's the next best thing to petting. To that end, introduce the brush, nail clippers and toothbrush when he is just a pup. Dogs who have not experienced these ministrations early in life may object when they are older…and bigger…and better able to resist. Grooming will then become a distasteful chore, even a battle, rather than a routine procedure that both of you can enjoy. The moral here is: start young!

Hold your first grooming session as soon as your Golden has adjusted to his new home base. Start with tiny increments of time, stroking him

Whether for an official bath, for a hose-down on a summer day or just filled with cool water in the hot weather, a kiddie pool gives your Golden his own personal oasis in the back yard. He will love it!

Make nail clipping a gentle experience for your Golden pup and he will grow into an adult who sits politely for his pedicures.

gently with a soft brush, briefly handling his paws, looking inside his ears, gently touching his gums. Use lots of encouraging sweet talk ("Ooh, what pretty ears!") and offer little bits of dog treats during each session, so he'll think such personal contact is a prelude to a feast. Ah, the power of positive association.

The adult Golden has a medium-length double coat, with an undercoat that varies in density depending on the climate in which the dog is raised. Regular brushing will remove dust and distribute the oils that will keep his coat clean and conditioned, with more frequent brushing needed during shedding seasons. Invest in a good book or even a video on grooming double-coated breeds. You will learn all of the tricks and shortcuts for maintaining a healthy, shiny coat.

How often should you bathe your Golden? Frequent bathing is seldom necessary and, in fact, will remove the essential oils that keep your dog's skin supple and his coat soft, gleaming and, most importantly, water-repellent. Bathe him every couple of months if you brush him regularly, more often if he plays in mud holes and rolls around in foul-smelling things (a favorite Golden pastime.)

Of course, there are those times when a bath is necessary. The bathing routine can be a challenge if your dog dislikes getting lathered up, although he shouldn't mind the water. To minimize the stress and struggle of bath time, start when your pup is small. Imagine wrestling a 60-pound adult into the tub or shower stall.

Lure your puppy into the tub with the usual food rewards, or maybe something extra-special like squirt cheese or peanut butter. Line the tub or shower with a towel for safe footing. Start with a dry tub, and after pup is comfortable there, gradually add shallow water and the bathing process. He may never learn to love it, but all you need is cooperation.

After shampooing, always be sure to rinse the coat and drying to prevent chilling. Spritz-on dry shampoos are handy in case you need a quick clean-up to remove dirt and body odor.

Nails should be trimmed once a month. This is always the least favorite grooming chore and the one most often

A real natural beauty, the Golden Retriever is a true combination of form and function, mixing a keen talent for hunting with dramatic good looks.

completely to avoid any itching from residual shampoo. A good chamois is the ideal tool for drying, as it absorbs water like a sponge. Keep him away from drafts for a good while after bathing neglected. Early introduction will help make the process easier. Puppies do not naturally like pedicures, so do start nail clipping as soon as possible. The longer you wait, the less he will cooperate. Try to make it a positive experience so that he at least tolerates it without a major battle. Offer those puppy treats each time so puppy will associate clipping with food rewards.

At first you may have to settle on only one or two nails at a time to avoid a wrestling match. That's a good start. It is better to trim a small amount of nail more

the nail may bleed profusely. If you happen to snip a quick, you can stanch the bleeding with a few drops of a clotting solution, available from your veterinarian, or a styptic stick or powder. Keep it on hand; accidents happen.

Weekly ear checks are worth the proverbial pound of cure. My veterinarian checks the ears of every dog she examines and is appalled at

It's everything *and* the kitchen sink for these adorable Golden babies, getting their first bath.

frequently than trying to cut back a nail that has grown too long. Nip off the nail tip or clip at the curved part of the nail. Be careful not to cut the quick (the pink vein in the nail); that is quite painful, and

how many foul ears she sees and how many owners admit that they never check or clean their dogs' ears.

Ear infections are common to all breeds of dog, with some Goldens more prone to chronic ear infection than others. The Golden's ear flaps can prevent air flow and keep the ear canal moist for musty growths, especially in humid climates. Regular cleansing, especially after swimming, with a specially formulated ear cleanser from your vet will keep your dog's ears clean and odor-free. Use a cotton ball or pad to clean the ear flap and the folds of the inner ear, but do not probe deeply, to avoid injuring the ear drum. Symptoms of ear infection include redness and/or swelling of the ear flap or inner ear, a nasty odor or dark, waxy discharge. If your Golden digs at his ear(s) with his paw, shakes his head a lot, or appears to lose his balance, see your vet at once.

The two most common mistakes owners make when dealing with an ear infection are waiting too long to seek treatment and failing to treat the ear for the entire course of medication, which allows the infection to recur. Be proactive with your Golden's ear care—the better he'll hear you say, "Get out of the garbage!"

GROOMING YOUR GOLDEN RETRIEVER

Overview

- Grooming is a big part of every Golden owner's life, so it's best to accustom the pup to the routine early on.
- Regular brushing is essential, especially during the twice-yearly shedding periods. It's necessary to get all the way down to the undercoat to prevent tangles and rid the coat of dead hair.
- Bathing too often is not recommended, as it will ruin the natural water-repellent qualities so essential to the Golden's coat.
- Nail trimming and ear cleaning are also part of the grooming routine.

Keeping the Golden Active

Whether gaiting in the show ring or enjoying a walk or run by his owner's side, the Golden is best kept active alongside those he loves.

The original Golden Retriever hunted waterfowl in the icy waters of the Scottish mainland. Although the 21st-century Golden is more pet than hunter, he still has the enthusiasm and vitality of his ancestors and needs vigorous exercise and activities to channel all of that energy. You, the owner, will benefit as well, since a well-exercised dog is happily tired and less inclined to find mischievous outlets for his unexpended energy.

That said, bear in mind that

neither the Golden puppy nor adult will get proper exercise on his own. A brisk daily walk, better yet, two walks a day, will help keep your Golden fit and trim, as well as keep his mind stimulated through the sights and sounds of the neighborhood.

DOG WALKS

How long and how far to walk depends on your Golden's age, physical condition and energy level. A young Golden's bones are soft and still forming, and thus more vulnerable to injury during his first year of life. Youngsters should not be subjected to heavy stress. That means shorter walks and no games or activities that encourage jumping or heavy impact on his front or rear until he is past the danger age. Playtime with other puppies and older dogs should be supervised to avoid excessive wrestling and twisting until your pup's structure has matured. Swim-

Although a water retriever by nature, the Golden still requires a safe introduction to water. Once a puppy gets his paws wet, he should take to water like a fish!

The Golden Retriever's prized traits of loyalty, intelligence and trainability make him one of the most frequently used and best-loved breeds for service and assistance work.

CHAPTER 13

ming, whenever possible, is excellent exercise for all ages.

When and where to walk is as important as how long. On warm days, avoid walking during midday heat and go out during the cooler morning or evening hours. If you're a jogger, your adult Golden is the perfect running partner if he is

Up and over the dog walk, the Golden Retriever conquers this and other agility obstacles with ease.

in good physical condition. Jogging on turf or another soft surface is easier on your Golden's joints and feet. Just make sure that your dog is healthy and fully developed before joining you on your mile-plus run.

Those daily walks or runs are also excellent bonding sessions. Your Golden will look forward eagerly to his special

time with you. As a creature of habit, your dog will bounce with joy when he sees you don your cap, pick up his leash or rattle your keys.

OBEDIENCE CLASSES

Consider taking your exercise program to another level. Plan a weekly night out with your Golden and enroll in a class. Obedience, maybe agility...or both! The benefits of obedience class are endless. You will be motivated to work with your dog daily so you and your dog don't look unprepared at each week's class. You'll both be more active and, thus, healthier. Your dog will learn the basics of obedience, will be better behaved and will become a model citizen. Plus, he will discover that you really *are* the boss!

AGILITY CLASSES

Agility classes offer even more healthy outlets for Golden Retriever energy. He will learn to scale an A-frame ramp, race headlong through a tunnel, balance himself on a teeter-totter, jump onto and off a platform, jump through a hoop, zig-zag between a line of posts and more. Agility training should not begin until at least 12 months of age to limit impact on those growing bones and muscles. The challenge of learning to navigate the agility obstacles, and his success in mastering each one, will make you proud of both of you!

COMPETING IN OBEDIENCE AND AGILITY

You can take both of these activities one step further and show your Golden in obedience and agility competitions. Shows and trials are held year-round and are designed for all levels of experience. Find a club or join a training group. Working with other fanciers will give you the incentive to keep working with your dog. Check your breed club and the AKC websites for details and contact persons.

HUNT TESTS AND HUNTING

What better way to exercise and enjoy your Golden than doing what most Goldens love best…retrieving ducks and pheasants? A Golden's love of bird work can range from mild to wildly passionate, depending on his working ancestry, but almost every Golden will enjoy time spent working in the field. Both the AKC and the United Kennel Club (UKC) sponsor hunt tests, which are designed for the non-competitive sportsman who may or may not actually hunt. Your local breed or retriever club can refer you to groups who train specifically for such events. Rules and

A swim followed by a jog along the shoreline is sure to keep any Golden fit and happy.

regulations for hunt tests are available on the AKC and UKC websites. (www.akc.org and www.ukcdogs.com).

FIELD TRIALS

By far the most challenging and difficult of all sporting-dog events, field trials are for those stout hearts who have the time and money to compete against the very best. Labradors dominate the field-trial scene, and few Goldens can compete with the dozens of Labs who earn field championships every year. However, pedigree is the name of this game. If you hope to be successful in this ultimate competition, make sure you have a pup with outstanding credentials before you consider entering the field-trial world.

DOG SHOWS

Conformation showing is the most popular competitive canine activity for all breeds, and Goldens are among the most popular of show dogs. If you plan to show your Golden, make sure you look for a show-quality puppy and discuss your goals with the breeder. Most local breed clubs host confor-mation training classes and can

Flying through the air with grace, this Golden effortlessly completes a tire jump at an agility trial.

help novices get started with their pups. As with other types of competition, it's best to start when your Golden is young so he develops a good "ring" attitude.

STAYING ACTIVE TOGETHER
Competition aside, your Golden will be happiest when he is with people, especially children. He needs to be part of family activities and will be an eager participant in outdoor sports and indoor play. If any accolade befits the Golden, it's best friend and companion.

Dogs in conformation receive a thorough hands-on examination by the judge to ensure correct structure. This dog has his mouth examined for full dentition and the properly formed scissors bite.

KEEPING THE GOLDEN ACTIVE

Overview

- As a Golden owner, you have many choices of how to keep your versatile dog active. The Golden will most appreciate activities done with those he loves.
- Be careful of pup's growing frame; do not allow strenuous exercise, jumping or roughhousing until he is past the "danger" age.
- A Golden will enjoy good daily walks or even jogs once he is fully developed and in good condition.
- Obedience and agility classes can progress to competitive levels, at which the Golden has the potential to excel.
- Interested owners can pursue hunting with their Goldens, either for fun or at different levels of competition depending on how seriously you want to take it.
- The Golden makes a beautiful show dog, with a happy personality that makes him a joy to watch.

CHAPTER 14

Your Golden and His Vet

A good veterinarian is worth his weight in *gold*-en good health! He will be your puppy's doctor and good friend, and your canine health-care educator. Find a good one before you bring your puppy home. Ask your friends, check with the local kennel club and your breeder. A good vet will plan your puppy's long-term health-care program and help you become smarter about how to keep your Golden healthy.

Take your puppy to your veterinarian within the first few days of bringing him home. Show the vet any health records of shots and wormings from your breeder. He will conduct a

Your breeder will provide you with health and vaccination records for your pup, and the vet will take over from there. Discuss the vaccination program with your vet, ensuring that your pup is being protected in the safest way.

thorough physical exam to make sure that your Golden pup is in good health and will work out a schedule for vaccinations, micro-chipping, routine medications and regular well-puppy visits. A good vet will be gentle and affectionate with a new pup and do everything possible to make sure the puppy is not frightened or intimidated.

Vaccine protocol for puppies varies with many veterinarians, but most recommend a series of three "combination" shots given at three- to four-week intervals. Your puppy should have had his first shot before he left his breeder.

"Combination" shots vary, and a single injection may contain five, six, seven or even eight vaccines in one shot. Many breeders and veterinarians feel that the potency in high-combination vaccines can negatively compromise a puppy's immature immune system, so they recommend fewer vaccines in one shot or even

In addition to showing your dog that you love him, petting him often can also help you discover lumps, bumps or other abnormalities not evident to the eye.

Start dental care early on with your pup to ensure that he grows up with a healthy and strong bite, and also that he tolerates handling of his mouth.

separating vaccines into individual injections.

VACCINES

The vaccines recommended by the American Veterinary Medical Association (AVMA) include distemper, fatal in puppies; canine parvovirus, highly contagious and also fatal in puppies and at-risk dogs; canine adenovirus, highly contagious and high risk for pups under 16 weeks of age; canine hepatitis, highly contagious, pups at high risk. Vaccines no longer routinely recommended by the AVMA, except when the risk is present, are canine parainfluenza, leptospirosis, canine coronavirus, *Bordetella* (kennel or canine cough) and Lyme disease. Your veterinarian will alert you if there is a risk of these non-fatal diseases in your area so you can immunize accordingly.

Recent canine research suggests that annual vaccinations may actually be over-vaccinating and may be respon-sible for many of today's canine health problems. Mindful of that, the American Animal Hospital Association guidelines currently recommend that veterinarians and owners consider a dog's individual needs instead of automatically vaccinating every year. The veterinarian can run titer tests to check a dog's antibodies rather than routinely vaccinate for parvo or distemper.

Rabies vaccination is mandatory in all 50 states. However, for many years the rabies vaccine has been available in a one-year and a three-year shot. The obvious wise course would be to vaccinate every third year after the rabies booster (which is given one year after the puppy series). Some states and counties, however, still require annual rabies vaccination and residents have no choice.

Always ask your vet what shots or medications your dog is getting at each visit and what they are for. A well-informed dog owner is better prepared to raise a healthy dog. Keep a notebook or dog diary and record all health information, especially after every vet visit, so you won't forget it. Believe me, you will forget.

HEARTWORM

These parasites are worms that propagate inside your dog's heart and will ultimately kill your dog. Now found in all 50 states, heartworm is delivered through a mosquito bite. Even indoor dogs should take heartworm preventative, which can be given daily or monthly in pill form, or in a shot given every six months. Heartworm preventative is a prescription medication available only through your veterinarian. A heartworm test is required before the vet will dispense the medication.

FLEAS AND TICKS

Fleas and dogs are traditional enemies, and it's likely that you will wage flea battle sometime during your Golden's lifetime. Fortunately today there are several low-toxic effective flea weapons to aid you in your war against these pests.

Tick-borne diseases such as Lyme disease (borreliosis), ehrlichiosis and Rocky Mountain spotted fever are now found in almost every state and can affect humans as well as dogs. Dogs that live in or visit areas where ticks are present, whether seasonally or year-round, should be protected.

SUBTLE CHANGES

Your Golden's health is in your hands between his annual visits to the vet. Be ever-conscious of any changes in his appearance or behavior. Things to consider:

Has your Golden gained a few too many pounds or suddenly lost weight? Are his teeth clean and white or does he need some plaque attackers? Is he urinating more frequently, drinking more water than usual? Does he strain during a bowel movement? Any changes

CHAPTER 14

in his appetite? Does he appear short of breath, lethargic, overly tired? Have you noticed limping or any sign of joint stiffness?

These are all signs of serious health problems that you should discuss with your vet as soon as they appear. This is especially important for the senior dog, since even minor changes can be a sign of something serious.

SPAYING/NEUTERING

To spay or neuter is the best health-insurance policy you can give your Golden. Females spayed before their first heat cycle (estrus) have 90% less risk of several common female cancers and other serious female health problems. Males neutered before their male hormones kick in, usually before six months of age, enjoy zero to greatly reduced risk of testicular and prostate cancer and other related tumors and infections. Statistically, you will make a positive contribution to the pet overpopulation problem and to your dog's long-term health.

YOUR GOLDEN AND HIS VET

Overview

- Find a good vet before your pup comes home and have an appointment arranged within the first few days.
- Your vet will pick up with vaccinations where the breeder left off. Discuss the inoculation schedule with your vet.
- Parasite control includes protection against the various types of worms and external parasites like fleas and ticks.
- Know your Golden so that you are able to recognize changes in his behavior that might indicate health problems
- Spaying or neutering a Golden that is not to be shown or bred is a good health-insurance policy, preventing or reducing the risk of several types of cancers and other diseases.